Happy Baking!

Best, Nicole Weston

# The Baking Bites Cookbook

• • •

## Nicole Weston

Cover Photo by Nicole Weston, Cover Design by Rebecca Perez
Photography by Nicole Weston and Barbara Bella

Library of Congress Cataloging-in-Publication Data available.

ISBN - 10: 0-6153-2035-X
ISBN - 13: 9780615320359

Printed in China

Distributed by BakingBites.com
Los Angeles, California

# Contents

# Foreward

I've always thought no matter how many people switch to digital media for their books, there will always be a place in the kitchen for a cookbook. There's just something familiar about being able to lay out a book on the counter and work right from the recipe, making notes in an already bound volume that you can keep for years as a reference. There is also something to be said for not having to worry about spilling on an electronic device - whether it is your laptop or a digital book reader - as you measure ingredients, mix wet ingredients and sample cookie dough. My cookbooks, on the other hand, usually have a few smudges that they wear as badges of honor, signs that they contain good recipes.

So, while I will never tire of the versatility that the internet offers Baking Bites the website, I wanted to put together a book form of Baking Bites that could join the other cookbooks on the shelf. Naturally, I needed to do a little bit of editing, since Baking Bites covers everything from reviews of cooking gadgets to recipes. I ended up selecting just a handful of recipe categories - the most popular on the site - for this book and creating a batch of completely new recipes to include. They're things like cookies and muffins, easy to make recipes that you can make again and again. I couldn't resist throwing in a couple of my favorites from the site because I turn to them again and again, as do many readers.

I hope that you enjoy some of these recipes as much as I do, and that this cookbook acquires a few smudges of its own as you bake your way through it.

-Nicole

Cookies

# Brown Butter Chocolate Chip Cookies

¾ cup butter, room temperature

⅔ cup sugar

⅔ cup brown sugar

2 large eggs

1 tsp vanilla extract

2 cups all purpose flour

¼ cup quick cooking oatmeal (not instant)

½ tsp baking soda

1 tsp salt

2 cups chocolate chips

1 cup chopped, toasted walnuts

*Browned butter is made by cooking melted butter over a low heat until the milk solids in the butter begin to toast and brown. It has a lovely toasty flavor on its own, but this flavor translates well into baked goods that taste richer and more complex with the addition. These chocolate chip cookies are chewy and tender, with an almost toffee-like note from the browned butter. The interesting thing is that you can't quite put your ginger on what makes them so good if you don't know the secret ingredient, but people are likely to reach for a second or third as they try to figure it out.*

● ● ●

Preheat oven to 350F. Line a baking sheet with parchment paper.

Melt butter in a small saucepan and cook over low-medium heat until butter has turned an amber color and smells toasty, but not burnt. Butter will darken quickly once it begins to turn. Pour from saucepan, scraping all the browned bits from the bottom with a spatula, into a small bowl to cool for 10-15 minutes.

When the butter has cooled down, whisk butter, sugar, eggs and vanilla extract until smooth.

In a medium bowl, whisk together flour, oatmeal, baking soda and salt. Add to browned butter mixture and stir until just combined. Stir in chocolate chips and walnuts.

Drop dough by rounded tablespoons, or 1-inch balls, onto prepared baking sheet.

Bake for 12-15 minutes, until cookies are light golden brown.

Cool for about 5 minutes on the baking sheet, then transfer to a wire rack to cool completely.

*Makes 3- 3½ dozen*

# Oatmeal Coconut Cookies

¾ cup butter, melted and cooled

⅓ cup sugar

1 cup brown sugar

2 large eggs

2 tsp vanilla extract

2 cups all purpose flour

1 tsp salt

½ tsp baking soda

1½ cups quick cooking oatmeal (not instant)

1 cup shredded coconut, sweetened or unsweetened

*Classic oatmeal cookies are one of my favorite types of cookies, especially when some raisins are added in for extra sweetness and chewiness. Shredded coconut has a similar effect in these cookies, making them a little bit sweeter and a little bit more chewy than the oatmeal cookies would be on their own. Unlike the raisins, however, the coconut is distributed throughout the cookie, so you'll get some in every bite. It's a great twist on a classic, especially if you're a fan of coconut.*

● ● ●

Preheat oven to 350F. Line a baking sheet with parchment paper.

In a large bowl, whisk together butter and sugars. Whisk in eggs, one at a time, followed by vanilla extract.

In a small bowl, whisk together flour, salt and baking soda. Pour into butter mixture and stir until well-combined. Stir in oats and coconut until dough is uniform.

Drop 1-inch balls of dough onto prepared baking sheet. Press each ball down lightly to flatten slightly and make the dough a uniform thickness.

Bake for 10-13 minutes, until cookies are lightly browned.

Transfer to a wire rack to cool completely.

*Makes 3 dozen*

# Double Chocolate Chip Cookies

2 cups semisweet or bittersweet chocolate chips, divided

1½ cups all purpose flour

½ cup cocoa powder

1 tsp baking soda

½ tsp salt

¾ cup butter, room temperature

1 cup sugar

2 large eggs

1½ tsp vanilla extract

*Who doesn't love a deep chocolate brownies? These cookies capture the same intense chocolate flavor as a batch of regular brownies, but in a single-serving form. The cookie dough has both cocoa powder and melted chocolate in it. The cocoa powder adds intensity to the chocolate flavor, while the melted chocolate adds richness. The cookies also have plenty of extra chocolate chips stirred in to ensure that you get plenty of chocolate with each bite. The finished cookies are rich, chewy and will satisfy just about any chocoholic. I recommend keeping a glass of milk on hand for eating these.*

● ● ●

Preheat oven to 350F. Line a baking sheet with parchment paper.

In a small bowl, melt (in the microwave or over a double boiler) ½ cup chocolate chips. Set aside to cool slightly.

In a medium bowl, sift together flour, cocoa powder, baking soda and salt. Set aside.

In a large bowl, with an electric mixer, cream together butter and sugar until light and fluffy. Add in eggs one at a time, beating until each is incorporated. Add in the vanilla and the melted chocolate.

Gradually blend in the flour mixture, followed by the remaining 1½ cups chocolate chips. Mix only until no streaks of the flour mixture remain. Drop by 1-inch balls onto the prepared baking sheet.

Bake at 350F for 9-11 minutes, until set.

Allow to cool on pans for 4-5 minutes before transferring to a wire rack to cool completely.

*Makes 3½ - 4 dozen*

# Coffee Cinnamon Snickerdoodles

## Topping

¼ cup sugar

2 tsp ground cinnamon

½ tsp cocoa powder

## Cookies

1½ cups sugar, divided

1 tsp ground cinnamon

½ tsp cocoa powder

2½ cups all-purpose flour

2 tsp cream of tartar

1 tsp baking soda

½ tsp salt

1 cup butter, room temperature

2 large eggs

1 tbsp instant coffee powder

½ tsp vanilla extract

½ tsp coffee extract (optional)

*A snickerdoodle is a vanilla sugar cookie that is rolled in cinnamon sugar before baking. They're classics because the relatively plain flavor combination appeals to just about everyone. This variation on the traditional recipe incorporates coffee into the cookie itself, for a more grown-up flavor. Adding coffee extract will boost the coffee flavor further, but it is optional if you don't have it on hand. A touch of unsweetened cocoa powder in the topping mixture helps to bring out some of the coffee notes in the cookies.*

• • •

Preheat the oven to 375F. Line a baking sheet with parchment paper.

**Make the topping:** In a small bowl, combine ¼ cup sugar and the ground cinnamon. Place in a medium-sized, shallow dish or bowl. Set aside.

**Make the cookies:** In a medium bowl, whisk together flour, salt, cream of tartar and baking soda.

In a large bowl, cream remaining 1½ cups sugar and butter together until fluffy. Beat in eggs one at a time, then blend in the instant coffee powder, vanilla extract and coffee extract, if using. Beat until mixture is very smooth and uniform in color. Stir in flour mixture.

Shape dough into 1 inch balls and roll in sugar-cinnamon-cocoa mixture. Place on baking sheet, leaving 2 inches between balls to allow for spreading.

Bake for for about 10 minutes, until very slightly browned on the edges.

Cool for 2-3 minutes on the baking sheet, then transfer cookies to a wire rack to cool completely.

*Makes 3½ - 4 dozen*

# Cornmeal Cranberry Walnut Cookies

1 cup butter, room temperature

½ cup brown sugar

1 tsp vanilla extract

1 ½ cups all purpose flour

½ cup yellow cornmeal

¼ tsp ground cinnamon

½ tsp salt

⅔ cup toasted walnuts, chopped

½ cup dried cranberries

*Cranberries and walnuts are very complimentary foods. Cranberries have a tart-sweet taste and walnuts have a slightly bitter, buttery taste. When they come together, the combination is bright and buttery at the same time. It is showcased well in this buttery slice-and-bake cookie. The butter cookie dough has some cornmeal added to it, which adds an incredibly delicate texture to the cookie, but otherwise mostly serves to highlight the fruit and nut combination. These cookies are very versatile and you can add extra spices or citrus zests to them for variety; the small amount of cinnamon in the dough just helps to round out the flavors. The dough can also be made well in advance and will store for at least several weeks in the freezer.*

● ● ●

In a large bowl, cream together butter and brown sugar. Mix in vanilla extract, flour, cornmeal and salt, mixing just until no streaks of flour remain. Stir in toasted, chopped walnuts and dried cranberries.

Form dough into a ball and place on a sheet of wax paper. Using your hands, shape the dough into a log about 2 inches across or a little less. Wrap in plastic wrap and chill in the fridge for about 2 hours, or in the freezer until you're ready to use it.

Preheat oven to 350F.

Using a sharp knife, cut chilled dough into slices that are no more than ¼-inch thick. Allow the dough to soften in the refrigerator if using frozen dough. Arrange on a parchment-lined baking sheet. Cookies will not spread very much, so you don't need to leave too much room between them.

Bake for 12-15 minutes, until cookies are lightly browned around the edges.

Cool on sheet for 2-3 minutes, then transfer to a wire rack to cool completely.

*Makes 3 dozen*

# Vanilla Browned Butter Sugar Cookies

½ cup butter, room temperature

½ vanilla bean

1 cup all purpose flour

½ tsp baking powder

¼ tsp salt

1 cup sugar

1 large egg

1 tsp vanilla extract

*Sugar cookies are often plain cookies, mild and sweet without too many extra flavors or textures. This variation is another cookie recipe that uses browned butter to add a whole new dimension to a basic cookie. The browned butter makes the cookies taste richer and much more buttery than they are. It also changes the texture of the cookies by making them a little firmer and chewier than a cookie made with the standard creaming method, where butter and sugar are beaten together before other ingredients are added. I infused the browned butter with vanilla by scraping the seeds from a vanilla bean into the saucepan as the butter browned, which boosts the vanilla flavor of the cookies and gives them a subtle, speckled look with the addition of the vanilla seeds.*

●　●　●

Preheat oven to 350F. Line a baking sheet with parchment paper.

Add butter to a small saucepan and cook over low-medium heat until butter begins to melt. Cut vanilla bean in half lengthwise and scrape seeds out of the pod and into the saucepan.

Continue to cook butter until it has turned an amber color and smells toasty, but not burnt. Butter will darken quickly once it begins to turn golden. Pour from saucepan, scraping all the browned bits from the bottom with a spatula, into a small bowl to cool for 10-15 minutes.

In a medium bowl, whisk together flour, baking powder and salt.

In a large bowl, whisk together sugar, egg and vanilla extract. Add in cooled, melted butter. Stir in flour mixture, mixing only until no streaks of flour remain.

Drop by 1-inch balls onto prepared baking sheet.

Bake for 10-12 minutes, until the edges are set and just start to brown.

Cool cookies on a wire rack.

*Makes 2 dozen*

# Dark Chocolate Pistachio Biscotti

2¼ cups all purpose flour

¼ cup cocoa powder

½ tsp baking soda

½ tsp baking powder

½ tsp salt

3 large eggs, room temperature

1 cup sugar

1 tsp vanilla extract

½ cup dark chocolate, chopped

½ cup toasted pistachios

*The two best things about biscotti are that they keep very well and they go great with both coffee and tea. This means that you can make a big batch, stick the cookies in an airtight container, and keep then around for snacking for weeks. That is, you can keep them if they last that long! These chocolate biscotti are crispy, perfect for dipping, and not too sweet. They have a nice dark chocolate flavor, thanks to the unsweetened cocoa powder in the dough, and are accented with chunks of dark chocolate and bright green pistachios.*

● ● ●

Preheat oven to 350F. Line a baking sheet with parchment paper.

Sift together flour, cocoa powder, baking soda, baking powder and salt in a medium bowl.

In a large bowl, use a hand mixer to beat eggs and sugar at medium speed until mixture is smooth and fluffy, 2-3 minutes. Stir in vanilla extract. At low speed or by hand, stir in flour mixture followed by chopped dark chocolate (or chocolate chips) and pistachios.

Drop spoonfuls of batter into long lines on prepared baking sheet and, with well floured hands, shape the irregular lines into rectangular logs about 1/2 inch high and about 4-inches across. Use more than one baking sheet, if necessary.

Bake for 20 minutes, until logs are set and firm at the edges. Logs will spring back slightly when the center of the log is lightly touched with a fingertip.

Slice logs into ⅓-½ inch thick slices and lay flat on baking sheet.

Lower oven temperature to 300F. Bake sliced cookies for 15 minutes, flip them and bake for an additional 15 minutes. If cookies are not firm, turn once more and bake for 10 more minutes.

Remove to a wire rack to cool. Store in an airtight container.

*Makes 4 dozen*

# Swirled Nutella Cookies

1 ¼ cups all purpose flour

½ teaspoon baking soda

½ teaspoon salt

½ cup butter, room temperature

1 cup brown sugar

1 large egg

½ cup Nutella

3 tbsp finely chopped hazelnuts

¼ cup Nutella

*Nutella is a chocolate hazelnut spread that is widely popular in France and Europe, but not quite as well know in the US. It's easy to eat by the spoonful, but it has a great flavor that goes well in all kinds of other dishes, too. I've had many Nutella cookies before and most of them play up the chocolate aspect, drowning out some of the nuttiness of the hazelnuts in the spread. This one doesn't do that. Not only are a few chopped hazelnuts added in for texture, but some Nutella is swirled into the cookie dough before baking. The cookies are thin and a bit chewy, and end up with a nice balanced Nutella flavor.*

● ● ●

Preheat oven to 350F. Line a baking sheet with parchment paper.

In a medium bowl, whisk together flour, baking soda and salt.

In a large bowl, cream together butter and brown sugar until mixture is light and fluffy. Beat in egg and ½ cup Nutella. Stir flour mixture and chopped hazelnuts into the batter, mixing only until no streaks of flour remain.

Add remaining ¼ cup Nutella to the cookie dough and gently swirl it through with a spatula or a butter knife. You should still see streaks of Nutella in the dough.

Drop by 1-inch balls onto prepared baking sheet.

Bake for 11-13 minutes, until cookies are set around the edges.

Cool on wire rack.

*Makes 2½ - 3 dozen*

# Mint Chocolate Sandwich Cookies

## Chocolate Mint Cookies

2 cups all purpose flour

¼ cup cornstarch

¼ cup cocoa powder

½ tsp salt

½ tsp baking soda

1 cup sugar

¾ cup butter, room temperature

¼ cup milk

1 tsp peppermint extract

## Chocolate Mint Ganache

8-oz semisweet chocolate chips

2 tbsp butter, room temperature

1 tsp peppermint oil

*There is something refreshing about the way that mint clears the palate, and even though there is something nice about the way that the flavor of chocolate lingers in your mouth after you eat some, it's hard to resist the combination of mint and chocolate that gives you the chocolate flavor and the clean finish. These chewy chocolate mint cookies are sandwiched around a mint chocolate ganache. The filling stays soft and rich after it sets up. I like a thin layer, but you can easily increase the amount the filling if you want to over-stuff your cookies with more chocolate.*

• • •

Make the cookies: In a medium bowl, sift together flour, cornstarch, cocoa powder, salt and baking soda.

In a large bowl, cream together sugar and butter until fluffy. Blend in half of the flour mixture, followed by the milk and peppermint extract. Blend in remaining flour mixture, mixing only until no streaks of flour remain visible.

Drop dough onto a large sheet of wax paper and shape into a log 1½ to 2-inches in diameter. Roll tightly to seal. Refrigerate dough for at least 2 hours, until very firm.

Preheat oven to 350F. Line a baking sheet with parchment paper.

Using a sharp knife, slice frozen dough into rounds no more than ¼-inch thick and place on baking sheet.

Bake for 9-11 minutes, or until cookies are set around the edges.

Cool completely on a wire rack.

Make the ganache: In a medium sized, microwave safe bowl, combine butter and chocolate chips. Heat in microwave in 30-60 second intervals, stirring frequently, until chocolate is very smooth.

Place 2-3 teaspoonfuls of ganache between pairs of cookies and sandwich them together. Allow cookies to cool to room temperature before storing.

*Makes 3 dozen cookies, 1 ½ dozen cookie sandwiches*

Bar Cookies
& Brownies

# White Chocolate Brownies

¼ cup butter

6 oz white chocolate, chopped

2 large eggs

I cup sugar

2 tsp vanilla extract

I cup all purpose flour

¼ tsp baking powder

½ tsp salt

6-oz dark chocolate chunks (1½ cups)

*Dark chocolate might be more commonly used when it comes to brownies, but white chocolate makes a fantastic brownie all on its own. White chocolate is smooth and creamy, and since it is milder than darker chocolates, you can really taste the vanilla in the recipe. I tossed in some some dark chocolate chunks for a bit of a contrast, but regular chocolate chips will make a good substitution for the dark chocolate if you prefer to use them. The brownies turn out to have the same rich and chewy texture that you'd find in a traditional chocolate brownie.*

• • •

Preheat oven to 350F. Line a 9-inch square baking pan with aluminum foil and lightly grease.

In a small bowl in the microwave, melt together butter and white chocolate. Stir until smooth. Set aside to cool slightly.

In a large bowl, beat together eggs, sugar and vanilla extract. Stir in cooled chocolate mixture.

Sift flour, baking powder and salt over the chocolate mixture and stir until just combined and no streaks of flour remain. Stir in chocolate chunks, then pour batter into prepared pan.

Bake for 30-35 minutes, until a toothpick inserted into the center comes out clean and the brownies are a light golden brown.

Cool in pan on a wire rack before slicing.

*Makes 25*

# Zebra Cheesecake Brownies

## Brownies

½ cup butter

2-oz dark chocolate, chopped

1 cup sugar

2 large eggs

1 tsp vanilla extract

⅔ cup flour

2 tbsp cocoa powder

¼ tsp salt

## Cheesecake

8-oz cream cheese,
room temperature

⅓ cup sugar

1 large egg

½ tsp vanilla extract

*Cheesecake brownies usually involve a layer of cheesecake baked on top of a layer of brownie batter. This version is almost just like that - only with lots more layers. To make the zebra pattern, you simply place small scoops of cheesecake batter on top of small scoops of brownie batter, allowing the batter to spread and fill the pan on its own. Layering scoop after scoop in this way creates a very unusual striped pattern in the finished brownies. Not only does it look great, but you end up with just the right amount of brownie and cheesecake in each bite. I like to cut these into fairly large pieces so the pattern is most visible, but the brownies are rich and smaller, bite-sized pieces might be better for sharing.*

● ● ●

**Make brownie batter:** Preheat oven to 350F. Line an 8×8-inch square baking pan with aluminum foil and lightly grease.

In a small, heatproof bowl, melt butter and chocolate together. Stir with a fork until very smooth. Set aside to cool for a few minutes.

In a large bowl, whisk together sugar, eggs and vanilla extract. Whisking steadily, pour chocolate mixture into sugar mixture. Stir until smooth. Sift flour, cocoa powder and salt into the bowl and stir until just combined. Set aside.

**Make cheesecake batter:** In a medium bowl, beat cream cheese, sugar, egg and vanilla extract until smooth.

Using a ¼ cup measure, drop a dollop of brownie batter into the center of the prepared pan. Using another ¼ cup measure, drop a dollop of the cream cheese batter into the center of the brownie batter. Repeat, alternating brownie batter and cream cheese batter until all batter has been used. Allow the batter to spread by itself as you work, don't try to manipulate it or you might loose the zebra effect.

Bake for 35-40 minutes, until brownies and cheesecake are set.

Cool in the pan completely before slicing and serving, either at room temperature or chilled. Brownies can be refrigerated, covered, for several days.

*Makes 16*

# Apple Oat Cobbler Squares

1 cup all purpose flour

½ cup rolled oats

½ tsp baking powder

1 tsp ground cinnamon

¼ tsp freshly ground nutmeg

¼ tsp salt

1 cup brown sugar

½ cup butter,
room temperature

1 large egg

1 tsp vanilla extract

2 medium apples, peeled and
diced (2 cups)

½ cup raisins or currants

½ cup chopped walnuts,
optional

*If apple cobbler, a baked dish that consists of apples topped with a sweetened, biscuit or cake-like topping, is an easier version of apple pie, these bars are just an easier version of apple cobbler. The bars have a spicy, oat-filled cake base that is absolutely packed with diced apples. In fact, there is just enough batter to hold the apples in place and very little more. The bars are moist, sweet and tender. They pack up well, so they make good snacks, but they can also easily stand in for a regular apple cobbler and get served warm, with a scoop of vanilla ice cream. Walnuts and raisins both make good additions to these squares if you like a little variety in your cobbler, although you can't go wrong with apple on its own, either.*

● ● ●

Preheat oven to 350F. Lightly grease an 8 or 9-inch square baking pan.

In a small bowl, whisk together flour, oatmeal, baking powder, spices and salt.

In a large bowl, cream together brown sugar and butter until light and fluffy. Beat in egg and vanilla extract, then stir in the flour and spice mixture, mixing only until no streaks of flour remain. Add in the diced apples, along with the raisins and walnuts, if using.

Pour batter into prepared pan.

Bake for 35-40 minutes, until apples are tender and a toothpick inserted into the center comes out clean.

Cool on a wire rack before slicing and serving.

*Makes 16*

# Orange Ricotta Cheesecake Bars with Chocolate Crust

## Crust

1/3 cup sugar

1/2 cup butter, softened

1 1/4 cups all-purpose flour

1/4 cup cocoa powder

1/4 tsp salt

## Cheesecake

1/2 cup sugar

1/2 cup milk

1 (8-oz) package plain cream cheese, softened

1 cup ricotta cheese

3 large eggs, room temperature

1 tbsp all purpose flour

1 tsp vanilla extract

1 tbsp orange zest

*Ricotta cheese is often added to cheesecakes to lighten the texture and make the cheesecakes seem a little bit fluffier, as opposed to being heavy and dense. It definitely does that here, so these cheesecake bars don't seem as weighty as a big slice of cheesecake would be. Still, the cheesecake portion of the bars is creamy and has a little bit of a creamsicle flavor from the vanilla extract and orange zest added into the batter. I use a chocolate shortbread crust for these cheesecake bars because orange and chocolate are always a good combination, as is chocolate and cheesecake. The best thing about the crust is that the filling can be poured on while the crust is still hot, so there is no down time waiting for the crust to cool completely before finishing up the recipe.*

● ● ●

**Make the crust:** Preheat oven to 350F. Lightly grease a 9×9-inch baking pan.

In a large or extra-large bowl, cream together sugar and butter, until smooth and fluffy.

Sift together flour, cocoa and salt in a small bowl. Working at a low speed, gradually beat flour mixture into butter mixture. Dough will be crumbly when all the flour has been incorporated. Press evenly into prepared pan and bake for 15-17 minutes, until lightly browned around the edges.

**Prepare the filling:** While the crust bakes, combine sugar, half & half and cream cheese in the bowl of a food processor and process until smooth. Add in eggs one at a time, waiting until each in incorporated to add the next, followed by flour, vanilla and orange zest.

Pour the filling over the hot crust when it has finished baking. Return pan to oven and bake for 22-26 minutes, until the filling is set (the filling will not "jiggle" when you gently shake the pan).

Cool completely on a wire rack before slicing. Store bars in the refrigerator.

*Makes 20*

# Dulce De Leche Shortbread Squares

2¼ cups all-purpose flour

1 cup sugar

¼ tsp salt

1 cup pecans, finely chopped

1 cup butter, room temperature

1 large egg

¾ cup dulce de leche

*Dulce de leche is a thick, milk-based caramel sauce that is very popular in Mexican and South American desserts. It is made by caramelizing sweetened condensed milk, so it has a much milkier flavor than most caramels, and a deeper sweetness to it. One popular way it is used is as a filling for butter cookie or shortbread cookie sandwiches. I added a layer right into this shortbread recipe to get the same effect. Shortbread dough is spread into the bottom of a pan, spread with a generous amount of the dulce de leche, and topped with more cookie dough. Buttery pecans really work well with the flavor of the dulce de leche, as well as with the already buttery shortbread base of this recipe, and add a little bit of crunch to an otherwise very tender, slightly soft bar cookie.*

• • •

Preheat the oven to 350F. Line a 9-inch square baking pan with aluminum foil and lightly grease.

In a large mixing bowl, whisk together flour, sugar, salt and pecans, then stir in the butter and egg until mixture is crumbly, like coarse and wet sand. Set aside 2 cups of the mixture, and pour the remaining mixture into the bottom of the prepared pan. Press down gently, but firmly, into an even layer.

Spread dulce de leche over the shortbread layer. Sprinkle remaining crumbs evenly over the top. If the mixture is too wet to sprinkle, simply break it up with lightly floured fingers and evenly distribute it.

Bake for 40-45 minutes, until lightly browned.

Cool bars in the pan before slicing.

*Makes 24*

# Zesty Lemon Bars

## Crust

½ cup butter, room temperature

¼ cup sugar

1 ¼ cups all purpose flour

¼ tsp salt

2 tsp lemon zest

½ tsp vanilla extract

## Filling

1 ¼ cups sugar

4 large eggs

1 cup fresh lemon juice

1 tbsp fresh lime juice

1 tbsp lemon zest

¼ cup all purpose flour

½ tsp baking powder

¼ tsp salt

*Lemon bars should be bright and refreshing, much like drinking a big glass of lemonade. Also like lemonade, it's easy to lose some of the natural zestiness of the lemon when you start adding lots of sugar and other ingredients to the citrus fruit. I boost the flavor in these bars in two ways. First, I add some lemon zest into the crust to give it a little more flavor. Second, I add both lemon and lime juice to the filling. The lime adds some extra acidity to the filling, but doesn't stand out on its own because only a small amount is used. It simply serves to highlight the lemon flavors in the bar even more.*

● ● ●

**Make the crust:** Preheat oven to 350F. In a large mixing bowl, cream together butter and sugar with an electric mixer. Blend in flour, salt, lemon zest and vanilla until mixture resembles very coarse sand. Pour into a 9x13-inch baking pan and press into an even layer.

Bake for about 15-17 minutes, until edges are barely beginning to brown.

**Make the Filling:** Combine all filling ingredients in a food processor and whizz until smooth and well combined. Pour into hot crust when it has just finished baking and return to oven.

Bake for an additional 11-14 minutes, or until filling is set.

Cool lemon bars to room temperature, then refrigerate until cold before slicing. Finished bars can be dusted with powdered sugar just before serving, if desired.

*Makes 25*

# White Chocolate Oatmeal Crunch Brownies

## Crust

⅓ cup all purpose flour

¼ tsp baking soda

¼ tsp salt

½ cup brown sugar

¾ cup oatmeal

⅓ cup shredded coconut (sweetened or unsweetened)

⅓ cup butter, melted and cooled

## Brownies

⅔ cup all purpose flour

¼ tsp baking soda

¼ tsp salt

1½-oz white chocolate, chopped

¼ cup butter

⅔ cup sugar

1 large egg

2 tbsp milk

1 tsp vanilla extract

*It might seem like a strange idea to add a cookie base to a pan of brownies, but it's actually a great way to introduce some texture to brownies. These white chocolate brownies are not too sweet and have a wonderfully milky vanilla flavor to them. It pairs perfectly with the oatmeal cookie crust, which is chewy and just crispy enough to provide a great base for the brownies. The crust has both coconut and oatmeal in it, both of which go well with the chocolate, but still stand out on their own because the white chocolate doesn't have as strong of a flavor as a darker chocolate would.*

● ● ●

**Make cookie base:** Preheat oven to 350F. Line an 8-inch square baking pan with aluminum foil, for easy removal later.

In a medium mixing bowl, whisk together flour, baking soda, salt, brown sugar, oatmeal and coconut. Pour in melted butter and stir to combine. Pour into prepared 8-inch square baking pan (pan can be ungreased if not using foil). Bake for 12 minutes.

**Make brownie batter:** Whisk together flour, baking soda and salt in a small bowl.

In another small bowl, melt white chocolate and butter together in the microwave. Set aside to cool.

Whisk together sugar and egg until light colored. When butter mixture is no longer hot, stir it into the egg mixture. Stir in the flour mixture, milk and vanilla extract, whisking until no streaks of flour remain.

When cookie base comes out of the oven, gently pour brownie batter on top and spread it out carefully with a spatula or the back of the spoon. The crust will not be set yet, so try to be gentle as you move the batter towards the corners of the pan. Return to oven and bake for 30 minutes.

Cool completely on a wire rack before slicing.

*Makes 20*

# Toffee Almond Shortbread Bars

2¼ cups all-purpose flour

1 cup sugar

1 tsp salt

1 cup almonds, finely chopped

¾ cup butter, room temperature

1 cup chopped chocolate covered toffee candy bars

*The only thing better than an intensely buttery, melt-in-your-mouth shortbread is a buttery, melt-in-your-mouth shortbread that is loaded up with equally buttery toffee bits. Chopped up chocolate covered toffee candy bars, such as Heath bars, provide the buttery toffee that makes these bars so delicious. These bars are also extremely easy to make, less than 5 minutes once your butter has softened to room temperature. The ingredients are blended together into a very sandy dough, and the dough is pressed out directly into a pan.*

● ● ●

Preheat the oven to 350F. Line a 9-inch square baking pan with aluminum foil and lightly grease.

In a large mixing bowl, whisk together flour, sugar, salt and almonds, then stir in the butter until mixture is crumbly, like coarse and wet sand. An electric mixer can be used to make this step easier. Mix in almonds, then toffee chunks.

Pour mixture into prepared pan and spread into the corners of the pan. Press firmly down into an even layer.

Bake for about 40 minutes, until lightly browned around the edges.

While shortbread is still hot and still in the pan, cut into 30 bars (5x6). A knife or a firm, metal spatula can be used.

Cool bars in the pan before removing.

*Makes 30*

# Homemade Samoas Bars

## Cookie Base

½ cup sugar

¾ cup butter, room temperature

1 large egg

½ tsp vanilla extract

2 cups all purpose flour

¼ tsp salt

## Topping

3 cups shredded coconut (sweetened or unsweetened)

12-oz good-quality chewy caramels

¼ tsp salt

3 tbsp milk

10-oz dark or semisweet chocolate

*Caramel de Lites, also known as Samoas, are one of the most popular Girl Scout Cookie flavors. It's hard to wait all year for them to go on sale, but there is no need to wait for this bar cookie version. These bars have a buttery shortbread base that is topped with the caramel-coconut Samoas topping and chocolate. The shortbread is a little more tender than you'd find in the original cookie, but the flavors are unmistakable. The bars are put together in stages, and each layer has to be prepared and cooled before the next one can be applied, so it takes a little longer to put these bars together than most bar cookies do. Still, it takes much less time than waiting for a once a year sale, so a little patience in the kitchen is well worth it if you're a fan of the classic Girl Scout cookie.*

● ● ●

**Make The Cookie Base:** Preheat oven to 350F. Lightly grease a 9×13-inch baking pan, or line with parchment paper.

In a large bowl, cream together sugar and butter, until fluffy. Beat in egg and vanilla extract. Working at a low speed, gradually beat in flour and salt until mixture is crumbly, like wet sand. The dough does not need to come together. Pour crumbly dough into prepared pan and press into an even layer.

Bake for 20-25 minutes, until base is set and edges are lightly browned. Cool completely on a wire rack before topping.

**Prepare the Topping:** Preheat oven to 300. Spread coconut evenly on a parchment-lined baking sheet (preferably one with sides) and toast 20 minutes, stirring every 5 minutes, until coconut is golden. Cool on baking sheet, stirring occasionally. Set aside.

Unwrap the caramels and place in a large microwave-safe bowl with milk and salt. Cook on high for 3-4 minutes, stopping to stir a few times to help the caramel melt. When smooth, fold in toasted coconut with a spatula.

**Tip:** To save a few minutes when preparing this recipe, drizzle the coconut-topped bars with melted chocolate instead of dipping them. This method is quicker, uses less chocolate and is quite a bit less messy. You still get all the same flavors in the finished product.

Put dollops of the topping all over the shortbread base. Using the spatula, spread topping into an even layer. Let topping set until cooled.

When cooled, cut into 30 bars with a large knife or a pizza cutter (it's easy to get it through the topping).

Once bars are cut, melt chocolate in a small bowl. Heat on high in the microwave in 45 second intervals, stirring thoroughly to prevent scorching. Dip the base of each bar into the chocolate and place on a clean piece of parchment or wax paper. Transfer all remaining chocolate (or melt a bit of additional chocolate, if necessary) into a piping bag or a Ziploc bag with the corner snipped off and drizzle bars with chocolate to finish.

Let chocolate set completely before storing in an airtight container.

*Makes 30*

Cakes

# Marble Layer Cake

## Marble Cake

2¼ cups all purpose flour

1½ tsp baking powder

¼ tsp salt

10 tbsp butter, room temperature

1⅓ cups sugar

3 large eggs

1 large egg white

2 tsp vanilla extract

¾ cup milk

2-oz dark chocolate, melted and cooled

## Vanilla Frosting

1 cup butter, room temperature

2 tsp vanilla extract

3 tbsp milk

3 - 3½ cups confectioners' sugar

*Marble cakes may be the most versatile cakes of all, since they offer a compromise to those who like chocolate cake and to those who like vanilla cake. If you can't make up you're mind, they're just about perfect. Marbled layer cakes have an extra visual appeal to them. Not only can you not be sure what kind of swirl you'll end up with, but you'll have two layers of swirl in every slice. Both vanilla and chocolate frosting are good choices for a marble cake. Vanilla frosting seems to show off the contrast between dark and light a little more than a chocolate frosting, so I usually opt for vanilla.*

• • •

**Make the cakes:** Preheat oven to 350F. Lightly grease two 9-inch round cake pans and like with parchment paper, lightly greasing the top of the parchment, as well.

In a medium bowl, whisk together flour, baking powder and salt.

In a large bowl, cream together butter and sugar until mixture is light and fluffy. Mix in eggs, one at a time, followed by the extra egg white and the vanilla extract, beating until mixture is smooth.

Alternating wet and dry ingredients, add in the milk and flour mixture in 2-3 additions, ending with a final addition of the flour mixture.

Divide cake batter in half. Fold melted chocolate into half of the batter using a spatula and mixing until the chocolate is evenly incorporated.

Divide cake batter evenly into prepared round cake pans by adding large dollops of chocolate and vanilla cake batters, creating a marbled look. Use a spatula to gently smooth the batter towards the edge of the pan in an even layer.

Bake for 20-25 minutes, or until a toothpick inserted into the center comes out clean.

**49**

**Tip:** There is a great temptation to over-swirl a marble cake in an attempt to get a nice marble effect. Don't over mix the two batters, or you'll end up with a cake that is a single brownish color, rather than black and white. Dropping the batter in dollops into the pan, interspersing chocolate and vanilla, and running a knife quickly through the batters once will leave you with a great looking marble effect and clear definition between chocolate and vanilla.

Turn cakes out onto a wire rack and remove parchment paper, allowing them cool completely before frosting.

Cakes may be made a day in advance and stored, wrapped in plastic wrap, at room temperature.

**Make the frosting:** In a large bowl, combine butter, vanilla, milk and about 2 cups of the confectioners' sugar. Beat at medium-high speed until smooth. Gradually add in remaining confectioners' sugar until frosting is thick, smooth and easy to spread.

To assemble: Place one layer of cake on a serving platter or cake stand. Spread with a thin layer of vanilla frosting. Place second layer of cake on top of the first, and again spread it with a thin layer of frosting.

Using about ½ cup of the frosting, spread a very thin layer of frosting over the sides of the cake to create a crumb coat, and hold any loose cake crumbs in place. Use remaining frosting to create a smooth layer on the top and sides of the cake.

*Serves 10*

# S'mores Cake

## Graham Cracker Cake

½ cup butter, room temperature

1 cup sugar

3 large egg yolks

1 tsp vanilla extract

2 cups graham cracker crumbs

2 tsp baking powder

¼ tsp salt

1 cup milk

3 large egg whites, room temperature

## Milk Chocolate Frosting

8-oz milk chocolate, chopped

¼ cup half and half/cream

2 tbsp butter

2 tbsp corn syrup

## Marshmallow Filling

1 7-oz jar marshmallow creme

*This is one of my all time favorite summer cakes. It looks like a s'more and tastes like a s'more, but, of course, is actually a cake. The cake layers are made with graham cracker crumbs, so they have a great graham cracker flavor to go along with a moist texture. The filling is marshmallow creme or marshmallow fluff and milk chocolate frosting. A final layer of milk chocolate goes on to the top of the cake to finish it off.*

●   ●   ●

**Make the cake:** Preheat oven to 375F. Lightly grease two 9-inch cake pans with cooking spray or oil and line with parchment paper.

In a large bowl, cream together the butter and sugar until light. Beat in egg yolks and vanilla extract.

In a small bowl, whisk together graham cracker crumbs, baking powder, salt. Working in two or three additions, alternate stirring the graham cracker mixture and the milk into the butter mixture.

Beat egg whites to soft peaks in a clean, medium-sized bowl. Working in 2 or three additions, fold egg whites into graham cracker mixture, mixing until no streaks of white remain.

Divide evenly into prepared pans.

Bake for about 20 minutes, or until cake springs back when lightly touched and a toothpick inserted into the center comes out clean.

Let cakes cool in pans for 3 minutes, then invert onto wire racks and remove parchment paper. Allow cakes to cool completely before filling and frosting.

**Make the frosting:** In a medium, microwave-safe bowl, heat chocolate, half and half, butter and corn syrup until melted. Stir with a fork or small whisk to ensure that everything comes together smoothly.

To assemble: Place one layer of cake on a cake stand or serving platter. Spread about ½ cup of the chocolate frosting onto the cake, then spread the marshmallow creme into an even layer.

Top marshmallow layer with second cake round, then pour remaining frosting over the top, spreading it into an even layer with an offset spatula and allowing it to drip slightly down the sides of the cake.

Cake will set up quickly, and should be stored in the refrigerator if not being served shortly after being assembled.

*Serves 8-10*

# Lime Poppyseed Bundt Cake

## Cake

3 cups all purpose flour

2 tsp baking soda

1 tsp salt

$\frac{2}{3}$ cup butter, room temperature

$1\frac{2}{3}$ cups sugar

1 tbsp lime zest

3 large eggs

1 cup sour cream

$\frac{1}{2}$ cup lime juice

2 tbsp poppy seeds

## Glaze

$1\frac{1}{4}$ cups confectioners' sugar

3 tbsp lime juice

1 tsp lime zest

*A little bit of lime juice goes a long way in this lime bundt cake. The cake has a bright citrus tang on its own, but the tart lime glaze really lets you get the most flavor from every slice. Two tablespoons of poppyseeds may not sound like much, but those little seeds have quite an impact on the appearance and texture of this cake. The seeds add a great speckled look to the interior of the cake. They also add a subtle crunch to the cake, and give the cake a more open crumb and a more tender texture.*

● ● ●

**Make the cake:** Preheat oven to 350F. Grease and flour an 10-inch bundt pan.

In a medium bowl, whisk together four, baking soda and salt.

In a large bowl, cream together butter, sugar and lime zest until light and creamy. Beat in eggs one at a time, waiting until each is fully incorporated to add the next.

Stir $\frac{1}{3}$ of the flour mixture into the butter mix, followed by the sour cream. Add another $\frac{1}{3}$ of the flour, then stir in the lime juice. Add the poppy seeds and all remaining flour, then mix just until no streaks of flour remain.

Pour into prepared bundt pan.

Bake for 45-50 minutes, until a toothpick inserted into the center comes out clean.

Cool in the pan for about 15 minutes, then turn the cake out onto a wire rack to glaze and cool.

**Make the glaze:** Whisk together sugar, lime juice and lime zest until pourable, but not runny. Add an additional tablespoon or two of sugar if the glaze is too thin. Drizzle over room temperature cake and allow glaze to set.

*Serves 12-16*

# Fresh Plum Cake

5 ripe plums

½ cup butter, soft

¼ cup brown sugar

½ cup sugar

1 large egg

1 tsp vanilla extract

1½ cups all purpose flour

2 tsp baking powder

¼ tsp salt

½ cup milk

1 tbsp coarse sugar, for topping

*Sometimes, the simplest cakes are the best. This cake needs no frosting and gets most of its flavor from the fresh plums that dot the top of it. I didn't peel my plums because plum skins are usually very thin and they add a gorgeous red color to the finished cake, as the purple of the skin becomes very vibrant during baking. This cake can be served warm or at room temperature. It's great plain, but also pairs well with a dollop of lightly sweetened whipped cream if you want to dress it up.*

● ● ●

Preheat oven to 350F. Line an 8-inch round cake pan with aluminum foil and lightly grease.

Halve all plums and remove the pits. Set aside.

In a large bowl, cream together butter and sugars. Beat in egg and vanilla.

In a medium bowl, whisk together flour, baking powder and salt.

With the mixer on low speed or by hand, alternate adding the dry ingredients and the milk to sugar mixture in 2 or 3 additions, ending with an addition of the flour mixture.

Pour into prepared pan and spread in an even layer. Arrange plum halves on the top of the cake, pressing them down into place gently. Sprinkle with coarse sugar.

Bake for 40-45 minutes, until a toothpick inserted into the center comes out clean and the plums are very tender.

Allow the cake to cool in the pan for 15-20 minutes, then use the foil to gently lift the cake out of the pan and place it on a cooling rack to cool before serving.

*Serves 8-10*

# Coffee Chiffon Cake

2 1/4 cups sifted cake flour

1 1/2 cups superfine sugar, divided

2 tsp baking powder

1/2 tsp salt

2/3 cup strong coffee, room temperature

2 tbsp Kahlua

1 1/2 tsp instant coffee powder

5 tbsp vegetable oil

1 tsp vanilla extract

6 large egg yolks

7 large egg whites, room temperature

*Chiffon cakes are tall and airy, as most of their structure comes from egg whites that are beaten and folded into the batter. Unlike other sponge cakes, chiffon cakes are very stable, thanks to the inclusion of some baking powder, and are very moist, a result of the addition of vegetable oil to the cake. The cakes keep well and will stay moist for days. This is a good feature in this coffee-flavored cake, because the flavors continue to meld as the cake sits. It includes brewed coffee, instant coffee and a dash of Kahlua.*

• • •

Preheat the oven to 325F. Get out a 10-inch tube pan, do not grease it.

In a very large bowl, whisk together flour, 1 1/4 cups of sugar, baking powder and salt. In a medium bowl, stir together coffee, Kahlua, vegetable oil, vanilla and egg yolks until very smooth, then pour into the dry ingredients and whisk just until no streaks of flour remain.

In another large bowl, beat the egg whites at low speed until they become slightly foamy. Bead in remaining 1/4 cup sugar, then increase mixer speed to high and beat egg whites to stiff peaks.

Gently stir one fourth of egg whites into the coffee mixture to lighten it. Then, gently fold the remaining beaten whites into the coffee mixture with a spatula until batter is uniform and no streaks of white remain.

Pour into the ungreased tube pan and bake for 55-60 minutes, until the top springs back when gently touched.

Invert cake over a bottle, or onto a wire rack if your pan has "feet" to hold it up, and let cool completely. When cooled, run a knife around the edges and turn cake out onto a serving platter.

*Serves 12-16*

# Blueberry Pound Cake

3 cups all purpose flour

1 tsp salt

2 tsp baking powder

1 cup butter, room temperature

2 cups sugar

4 large eggs

1 tbsp vanilla extract

1 cup buttermilk

2 cups fresh or frozen blueberries

*A good pound cake should be moist, tender and have a very tight crumb. This density is great when you want to mix something like chocolate chips, nuts or fruit into a cake batter because it helps hold the add-ins in place and doesn't let them sink to the bottom of the cake. Fresh or frozen blueberries work equally well in this cake. If you opt for frozen berries, there is no need to defrost them before adding them to the cake batter.*

● ● ●

Preheat oven to 325F. Grease and flour a 10-inch bundt pan.

In a medium bowl, whisk together flour, salt and baking powder.

In a large bowl, cream together butter and sugars until light and fluffy. Beat in eggs one at a time, waiting until each is fully incorporated before adding the next. Blend in vanilla extract.

Stir $\frac{1}{3}$ of the flour mixture into the butter mixture, followed by half of the buttermilk. Add another $\frac{1}{3}$ of the flour, then the rest of the buttermilk and the final portion of flour. Fold in blueberries gently with a spatula. If using frozen berries, toss with 2-3 tsp flour before adding to prevent them from streaking the batter with berry juice. Pour into prepared pan.

Bake for 70-75 minutes, until a toothpick inserted into the center of the cake comes out clean and the top springs back when lightly pressed.

Cool for 15 minutes in the pan, then turn the cake out of the pan on a wire rack to cool completely.

*Serves 12*

# Mexican Chocolate Black Bottom Cupcakes

## Cream Cheese Filling

16-oz cream cheese, room temperature

½ cup sugar

2 large egg whites, room temperature

2 tbsp milk

⅔ cup sweetened, shredded coconut, finely chopped

## Cake

1½ cups all-purpose flour

½ cup cocoa powder

1¼ cups sugar

½ tsp salt

1¼ tsp baking soda

1½ tsp ground cinnamon

¼ tsp ground cayenne pepper

¾ cup buttermilk

1⅓ cups water

½ cup butter, melted and cooled

1 tsp vanilla extract

¼ tsp almond extract

*Black bottom cupcakes fall somewhere between cupcake and muffin. They're rich and very chocolaty, but have no frosting. Instead, they have a cheesecake-like filling that is baked right into the cake itself. This variaion on the classic recipe is a mexican chocolate version of the cupcake, with cinnamon and cayenne pepper incorporated into the chocolate to give it a darker and spicier flavor. A little bit of coconut in the filling gives it a nice, chewy texture and helps highlight the nuttiness provided by a little bit of almond extract in the chocolate cake.*

• • •

Preheat oven to 350F. Line two 12-cup muffin pans with paper liners.

**Make the filling:** In a medium bowl, beat together cream cheese, sugar and salt until smooth. Blend in egg whites and milk, mixing until filling is well-blended. Set aside.

**Make the cake:** In a large bowl, sift together flour, cocoa powder, sugar, salt, baking soda and spices.

Make a well in the center and add in buttermilk, water, melted butter, vanilla extract and almond extract. Stir together until just combined and no streaks of flour remain.

Divide cake batter evenly among 24 cupcake liners. Top each portion of batter with 1 rounded tablespoon cream cheese mixture (there may be a bit of filling leftover).

Bake for 20-25 minutes. A toothpick inserted into the side (cake only part) should come out with a few moist crumbs on it. Rotate pans halfway through baking if you are using two racks.

Cool in pans for 5 minutes. Filling will sink slightly as the cakes cool. Remove cupcakes to wire racks to cool completely.

*Makes 24*

**63**

# Buttermilk Vanilla Cupcakes with Cream Cheese Frosting

## Cupcakes

1½ cups all purpose flour

1½ tsp baking powder

¼ tsp salt

⅓ cup butter, room temperature

¾ cup sugar

1 large egg

1½ tsp vanilla extract

1 cup buttermilk

## Frosting

8-oz cream cheese, room temperature

4-oz butter, room temperature

¼ cup milk

1 tsp vanilla extract

2½ - 3 cups confectioners' sugar

*I always like to use buttermilk in cakes, especially in vanilla cakes that can be a little one-dimensional on their own. Buttermilk really highlights the flavor of the butter in the cake, making it seem richer, and it also helps to keep the cake nice and moist. As for the frosting, cream cheese frosting is easily my favorite topping for just about any cupcake. It has more flavor than most plain chocolate and vanilla and never seems to taste too sugary even though it adds a lot of sweetness to the cupcake overall.*

●　●　●

**Make the Cupcakes:** Preheat oven to 350F. Line a 12-cup muffin tin with paper cups.

In a medium bowl, whisk together flour, baking powder and salt.

In a large bowl, cream together butter and sugar until light and fluffy. Beat in egg and vanilla extract.

Blend in about ⅓ of the flour mixture, followed by half of the buttermilk. Add in another ⅓ of the flour mixture, followed by the rest of the buttermilk and the remaining flour. Stir only until just combined and no streaks of flour remain.

Divide evenly into prepared baking cups, filling each about ¾ full.

Bake for 15-17 minutes, until a toothpick inserted into the center comes out clean and the top springs back when lightly pressed.

Cool on a wire rack before frosting.

**Tip:** If you want to turn the vanilla frosting into chocolate frosting, simply sift 1/4 cup of cocoa powder into the rest of the frosting ingredients and beat until well-combined. To make the vanilla frosting into a mocha frosting, add in the cocoa powder and replace the milk with 1/4 cup of strong coffee or espresso.

**Make the Frosting:** In a medium bowl, cream together cream cheese and butter until smooth. Beat in milk and vanilla, followed by 2 cups of the confectioners' sugar. Gradually blend in remaining sugar as needed until frosting is thick, smooth and spreadable.

Spread onto cooled cupcakes using an offset spatula or butter knife.

*Makes 12*

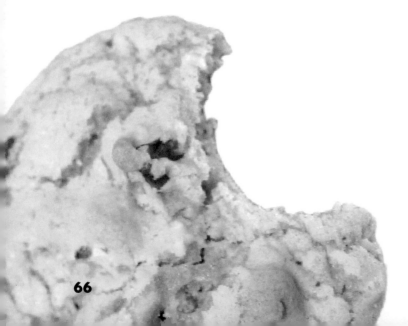

Pies &
Tarts

# Basic Pie Crust

## Double Crust Pie

2¼ cups all purpose flour

1 tbsp sugar

1 tsp salt

1 cup butter, chilled and cut into chunks

approx ⅔ cup cold water

## One-Crust Pie

1¼ cups all purpose flour

¼ tsp salt

1 tsp sugar

8 tbsp butter, chilled and cut into chunks

4-5 tbsp ice water

*Pie dough is surprisingly easy to make if you've never made it before. It's also fun to make, since the best way to put it together is to use your fingers to rub the butter in to the flour. It gets your hands messy and produces the best finished product, since rubbing the butter in evenly distributes it, but doesn't over distribute it to the point where you have a crumbly crust, instead of a flaky one. Crust can be made a few days in advance and stored in the refrigerator, tightly wrapped, until ready to use. It can also be frozen and defrosted in the refrigerator before using if you really want to make it ahead.*

● ● ●

Choose ingredient amounts for a double crust or one crust pie. The process is the same.

Whisk together flour, salt and sugar in a large bowl. Rub in butter with your fingertips until mixture is very coarse, but no pieces bigger than a large pea remain. Using a fork, stir in cold water until dough almost comes together into a ball (you might not need to use all the water, so add it in as you go). This process may be done in the food processor, as well, but take care not to over-blend the butter.

Divide dough in half and shape each half into a ball with your hands. Wrap each in plastic wrap. Chill in the refrigerator for at least 30-60 minutes before using.

**To prebake a single-crust pie:**
To prebake, preheat oven to 375F. Roll dough out to fit a 9-inch pie pan and trim the crust. Prick the bottom with a fork a few times. Line the inside of the crust with aluminum foil, not covering the edges, and fill with pie weights or about 2 cups of dried beans. Bake for 25 minutes, until very lightly browned. Remove foil and weights and bake for an additional 10 to 15 minutes, until medium brown at the edges. Set aside to cool.

# Apple Brown Betty Crumble Pie

dough for 9-inch pie crust

6 medium-large apples

1/4 cup sugar

1/2 tsp ground cinnamon

1/4 tsp ground allspice

2 cups fresh breadcrumbs

1/4 cup oatmeal, rolled
or quick-cooking

1/2 cup brown sugar

1/2 tsp ground cinnamon

1/8 tsp salt

3 tbsp butter, melted

*This pie combines two of my favorite apple desserts: Apple Brown Betty and Apple Pie. A brown betty usually has a topping made with fresh breadcrumbs that are sweetened and spiced before being mixed with fruit. I used a brown betty type of mix to make a very easy crumble topping for this pie. The topping bakes up to be a bit crispy and very flavorful. To make the fresh breadcrumbs, simply pulse a few slices of bread in the food processor. I like challah and brioche, but white and whole grain breads work well here, too.*

• • •

Preheat oven to 350F.

Roll out pie dough to fit a 9-inch pie plate and place into plate. Refrigerate until ready to use.

Peel and slice apples into 8-10 slices each. Place apples into a large mixing bowl, adding in sugar, cinnamon and allspice. Stir well and set aside.

In a medium bowl, stir together breadcrumbs, oatmeal, brown sugar, cinnamon and salt. Add in melted butter and stir with a fork until mixture resembles wet sand.

Add 1/4 cup of mixture to apple mixture and stir well.

Pour apple slices into prepared pie plate, spreading them into an even layer, and top with crumb mixture.

Bake for 45-50 minutes, until apples are tender when tested with a sharp knife and topping is browned. If topping becomes too dark, loosely tent a piece of foil over the pie during the last few minutes of baking.

Cool pie to room temperature before slicing.

*Serves 10*

# Fresh Strawberry Tart

## Crust

1 1/4 cups all purpose flour

1/4 cup sugar

1/8 tsp salt

1/2 cup butter, room temperature

1 large egg

1 tsp vanilla extract

## Filling

4-oz dark chocolate

8-oz cream cheese, room temperature

1/2 cup powdered sugar

2 tbsp Kahlua

1 pint fresh strawberries, trimmed and halved

1/2 cup seedless raspberry jam

*This strawberry tart incorporates several wonderful elements, the first and foremost being sweet, fresh strawberries that look like jewels on top of the tart. The tart base is tender and shortbread-like. It is sealed with a thin layer of dark chocolate that prevents the unbaked cream cheese filling, as well as the juices from the berries, from soaking into the crust and making it limp. A thin layer of melted raspberry jam is brushed all over the tart to finish it off, giving the berries a hint of extra sweetness and a ruby-red shine.*

● ● ●

**Make The Crust:** In a large bowl, whisk together flour, sugar and salt. Add butter and beat at a low speed until very coarse crumbs form. Add in egg and vanilla and beat for 2-3 minutes at low speed, or until dough comes together into a ball.

Transfer dough to a 9-inch tart pan and, after flouring your fingers, press it out into a thin, even layer along the bottom of the pan and up the sides. Make sure to press the dough down in the corners of the tart, as the corners do not need to be thick but the crust needs to fill both the corners and the flutes of the tart pan

**Make the Tart:** Melt 4-oz dark chocolate in a small, microwave-safe bowl and pour into crust. Spread evenly with a spatula or pastry brush to coat the bottom with a thin layer of chocolate.

Refrigerate for 30 minutes, or until chocolate is cool and firm.

Beat cream cheese, powdered sugar and Bailey's in a large bowl until smooth. Pour into cooled crust.
Top cream cheese filling with sliced berries.

In a small saucepan, heat the jam over medium heat until it is warm and liquid. Use a pastry brush to brush it over the strawberries

Refrigerate tart for at least 30 minutes, or until ready to serve.

*Serves 10*

# Plum Pie

1 recipe for double-crust pie dough

2 lbs fresh plums
(8-10, depending on size)

1 cup sugar

¼ cup cornstarch

¼ tsp salt

2 tsp vanilla extract

2 tbsp milk

4 tbsp coarse sugar

*Plum pie was a recipe I stumbled onto by accident when I had a surplus of plums and needed to do something that would use up quite a few at onceThe pie quickly became a favorite and I started to make it over and over again.The plums are sweeter than peaches and other stone fruits that typically work their way into pies, so this dish has an almost berry-like taste to it. It also has a berry-like color because the plums are not peeled before adding them to the pie and imbue the filling with a deep purple-red color.*

● ● ●

Preheat oven to 375F.

Wash plums and cut in half, removing the pits. Cut about half of the plums into quarters and half into sixths (the size variety helps them fit into the pie plate well). Place plums in a large bowl, add in sugar, cornstarch, salt and vanilla extract and stir well with a spatula. Set aside.

Roll out the bottom pie crust on a lightly floured surface, making sure there will be a bit of overhang around the edge of the pie plate, and transfer to pie plate. Fill pie crust with plum mixture. Roll out top pie crust, and lay on top of the pie plate, crimping or pinching edges to seal filling in completely.

Brush the top of the crust with milk and sprinkle with coarse sugar. Cut 5 or 6 slits in the top crust with a sharp knife.

Bake for 65-75 minutes, until crust is well browned and the filling is thick and bubbling through the vents on the top of the pie.

Cool pie on a wire rack completely before slicing, to allow the filling to set up.

*Serves 8*

# Chocolate Coconut Tart

## Crust

1¼ cups all purpose flour

¼ cup sugar

⅛ tsp salt

½ cup butter, room temperature

1 large egg

1 tsp vanilla extract

## Filling

½ cup sugar

1 large egg

2-oz bittersweet chocolate, melted and cooled

1 tbsp cocoa powder

1⅔ cup coconut milk

1 cup shredded coconut, sweetened or unsweetened

*The filling for this tart is non-dairy, made with coconut milk instead of regular milk or cream. This gives it a very smooth texture and a very clean finish, not to mention the fact that it really highlights the coconut and draws out its flavor through the chocolaty custard. Despite its deep flavor, the filling actually does not contain a large amount of chocolate, although the bittersweet chocolate and cocoa powder it does contain both add contribute a lot to that depth. The tart does not take long to make because the filling is added to the crust while it is still hot, you don't have to wait for the crust has cooled completely before you finish making the recipe, even though you do need to wait until the tart has cooled to serve it.*

• • •

Preheat the oven to 375F.

**Make the Crust:** In a large bowl, whisk together flour, sugar and salt. Add butter and beat at a low speed until very coarse crumbs form. Add in egg and vanilla and beat for 2-3 minutes at low speed, or until dough comes together into a ball.

Transfer dough to a 9-inch tart pan and, after flouring your fingers, press it out into a thin, even layer along the bottom of the pan and up the sides. Make sure to press the dough down in the corners of the tart, as the corners do not need to be thick but the crust needs to fill both the corners and the flutes of the tart pan.

Place a sheet of aluminum foil over the crust, press down gently to shape it to the tart, and pour in pie weights.

Bake pie crust for 15 minutes with the pie weights, then remove the foil and weights from the crust. Bake for an additional 10 minutes.

**Tip:** If you don't have pie weights, you can use dried beans or lentils when you prebake your pie or tart shell. After the beans cool down from their trip into the oven, store them in a ziploc bag; they can be reused to future pies.

**Make the Filling:** While the crust is baking, prepare the filling. In a large bowl, whisk together sugar and egg until smooth. Whisk in melted chocolate and cocoa powder, making sure no streaks of cocoa powder remain visible. Stir in coconut milk and shredded coconut.

When the crust is finished prebaking, remove it from the oven. Lower the oven temperature to 350F.

Pour filling into hot crust and place it back in the oven.

Bake for 45-50 minutes, or until lightly set. Filling should jiggle when pan is nudged, but should not look like a liquid. Filling will be softly set in the center.

Move pan to a wire rack and allow tart to cool completely before slicing. Tart will sink slightly as it cools. It can be served chilled or at room temperature.

*Serves 10-12*

Quickbreads
& Coffee Cakes

# Browned Butter Oatmeal Bread

½ cup butter, room temperature

2 cups all purpose flour

1 cup rolled oats

1 tsp baking powder

1 tsp baking soda

½ tsp salt

½ cup sugar

½ cup brown sugar

1 tsp vanilla extract

2 large eggs

1 ¼ cup buttermilk

*The flavor of browned butter is not only delicious, but it's difficult to isolate in a dish. The rich, nutty taste of toasted butter is unique and, while it makes a great addition to many baked goods, it doesn't always obviously stand out in the finished product. One of the great things about this quick bread is that the browned butter in it shines through in the finished loaf. The nuttiness of the butter is complemented perfectly with the nutty rolled oats in the bread, and the tight crumb seems to hold that flavor in so you get a burst of browned butter notes in every bite.*

• • •

Preheat oven to 350F. Grease and flour a 9x5-inch loaf pan.

Melt butter in a small saucepan and cook over low-medium heat until butter has turned an amber color and smells toasty, but not burnt. Butter will darken quickly once it begins to turn. Pour from saucepan, scraping all the browned bits from the bottom with a spatula, into a small bowl to cool for 10-15 minutes.

In a large bowl, whisk together flour, oats, bakin g powder, baking soda and salt.

In a medium bowl, whisk together sugars, vanilla extract, eggs and buttermilk until mixture is smooth. Whisk in cooled butter.

Stir butter mixture into flour mixture, stirring only until batter is just combined and no streaks of flour remain. Pour into prepared loaf pan.

Bake for 50-60 minutes, until a toothpick inserted into the center comes out clean.

Cool loaf in pan for about 10 minutes, then turn out onto a wire rack to cool completely before slicing.

*Makes 1 loaf*

# Cream Cheese Swirled Carrot Cake Loaf

## Cream Cheese Filling

8-oz cream cheese, room temperature

1 large egg white

¼ cup granulated sugar

½ tsp vanilla extract

## Carrot Cake

1¾ cups flour

1½ cups sugar

2 tsp baking soda

½ tsp salt

1 tsp ground cinnamon

½ tsp ground allspice

¼ tsp ground nutmeg

⅓ cup vegetable oil

2 large eggs

¼ cup buttermilk

1½ cups shredded carrots

*Some would say that the best part of a carrot cake is the cream cheese frosting. Others might say the moist texture of the cake and the interesting spices are the reason they'll reach for seconds. This loaf has both, all swirled together in one loaf, so it should suit people on both sides of the fence. The cake part of the loaf is simple and lightly spiced. It is fairly sweet, but provides a nice contrast for the not-too-sweet cream cheese layer, so there is a good balance in each slice. The filling is a little more dense than your average cream cheese frosting might be, so it will cause the cake to sink slightly in the center as the loaf cools down.*

● ● ●

Preheat oven to 350F. Lightly grease a 9x5-inch loaf pan. Line bottom of pan with a piece of parchment paper.

**Make the cream cheese filling:** In a medium bowl, beat together cream cheese, egg white, sugar and vanilla until smooth.

**Make the cake:** In a large bowl, whisk together flour, sugar, baking soda, salt and ground spices.

In a medium bowl, whisk together oil, eggs and buttermilk. Pour into dry ingredients and stir until just combined and no streaks of flour remain. Stir in shredded carrots.

Pour half of carrot cake batter into prepared pan. Spoon cream cheese mixture on top, spreading it into as even a layer as possible. Pour remaining carrot cake batter on top.

Bake for 60 65 minutes, or until a toothpick inserted into the center of the cake - not the filling - comes out clean and the top springs back when lightly pressed.

Cool in the pan for 15 minutes, then carefully turn the cake out, peel off the parchment paper, and reinvert the loaf onto a wire rack to cool completely before slicing.

*Makes 1 loaf*

# Chai-Spiced Crumb Coffee Cake

## Topping

$\frac{1}{3}$ cup sugar

$\frac{1}{3}$ cup brown sugar

1 tsp cinnamon

$\frac{1}{2}$ ginger

$\frac{1}{2}$ tsp cardamom

$\frac{1}{2}$ tsp allspice

$\frac{1}{4}$ tsp salt

1$\frac{1}{2}$ cups all purpose flour

$\frac{1}{2}$ cup butter, melted and cooled slightly

## Cake

1$\frac{3}{4}$ cups all purpose flour

$\frac{3}{4}$ tsp baking powder

$\frac{1}{2}$ tsp baking soda

$\frac{1}{4}$ tsp salt

$\frac{2}{3}$ cup butter, soft

1 cup sugar

2 large eggs

1$\frac{1}{2}$ tsp vanilla extract

$\frac{2}{3}$ cup sour cream, full or low fat

*Cinnamon is the standard spice for topping a crumb coffee cake. This coffee cake keeps the classic crumb topping, but spices it up a little more by adding in some of the same spices that are found in chai tea, including cinnamon, ginger, cardamom and allspice. These spices really help to make the coffee cake memorable - and they also make you want to come back for a second slice.*

● ● ●

Preheat oven to 350F. Line a 9-inch square baking pan with parchment paper or lightly greased aluminum foil.

**Make the Topping:** In a medium bowl, combine all topping ingredients except butter. Whisk to blend.

Gradually stir in the melted butter, using a large fork or spatula to mix. When all the butter has been incorporated and the mixture looks like wet sand, squeeze small clumps together to make large crumbs ranging in size from that of a pea to that of a grape. Set aside.

**Make the Cake:** In another medium bowl, whisk together flour, baking powder, baking soda and salt.

In a large bowl, cream butter and sugar together until light. Beat in eggs, one at a time, followed by vanilla extract. With the mixer set on a low speed (or by hand), alternately add in flour and sour cream in two or three additions. When no streaks of flour remain, pour into prepared pan. Top evenly with crumb mixture.

Bake at 350F for about 45 minutes, or until a toothpick inserted into the center comes out clean.

Cool on a wire rack before slicing.

*Serves 9-12*

**85**

# Coconut Banana Bread

2½ cups all purpose flour

2 tsp baking powder

½ tsp salt

½ tsp ground cinnamon

1 cup sugar

2 large eggs

1 cup mashed banana
(2 med-large)

½ cup coconut milk

¼ cup butter, melted

1 tsp vanilla extract

1 cup shredded coconut

*The combination of coconut and banana in a single loaf sounds like it would have a tropical flavor to it, but that's really not the case with this quick bread. Instead, it is just a banana bread with a twist. It has a rich banana flavor that is accented with sweet coconut and a hint of ground cinnamon. The coconut actually adds more in terms of texture than flavor, giving the bread a nice chewiness and breaking up the cake so that it is very tender as you eat it. This recipe does use coconut milk instead of regular milk, so it does have an extra little coconut note to it to help draw out the flavor of the shredded coconut. If necessary, you can substitute regular milk for the coconut milk and still have good results with this loaf.*

●　●　●

Preheat oven 350F. Lightly grease and flour a 9×5-inch loaf pan.

In a medium bowl, whisk together flour, baking powder, salt and cinnamon

In a large bowl, whisk together sugar and eggs until well combined, then whisk in the mashed banana, coconut milk, melted butter and vanilla extract. Pour dry ingredients into wet ingredients and stir until just combined, making sure no streaks of flour remain. Stir in shredded coconut and pour batter out into prepared baking pan.

Bake for 60 minutes, or until a toothpick inserted into the center comes out clean, or with only a few moist crumbs attached.

Turn loaf out onto a wire rack to cool completely before slicing.

*Makes 1 loaf*

# Fig, Cherry and Almond Loaf

2¼ cups all purpose flour

½ cup sugar

½ cup brown sugar

1 tsp baking soda

½ tsp baking powder

½ tsp salt

1 cup buttermilk

¼ cup vegetable oil

1 large egg

1 tsp vanilla extract

1½ cups chopped, fresh figs

½ cup dried cherries

¼ cup plus 2 tbsp sliced almonds, divided

2 tbsp coarse sugar

*Fresh figs are a very easy ingredient to work with. There is no need to peel or prep them in any way, just wash, chop and toss into a batter. Figs have a rich sweetness, a lot of moisture and a beautiful color to them, all of which help to make this a great quick bread recipe. I added in some dried cherries to complement the deep sweetness of the figs and some sliced almonds for a little bit of texture. The almonds make for a particularly nice crunchy topping that contrasts well with the softer, sweeter bread. I used mission figs for this recipe, but if you prefer another variety of fig, feel free to work with that instead.*

● ● ●

Preheat oven to 350F. Grease and flour a 9x5-inch loaf pan.

In a large mixing bowl, whisk together flour, sugar, brown sugar, baking soda, baking powder and salt.

In a medium bowl, whisk together buttermilk, oil, egg and vanilla extract until smooth. Pour into dry ingredients and mix just until no streaks of flour remain visible. Fold in chopped figs, dried cherries and ¼ cup almonds just until evenly distributed.

Pour into loaf pan and top with 2 tbps sliced almonds and a generous sprinkle of coarse sugar.

Bake for 55-60 minutes, until a toothpick inserted into the center comes out clean.

Turn loaf out onto a wire rack to cool.

*Makes 1 loaf*

# Grandma's Pear Cake

2 cups all purpose flour

2 tsp baking powder

1 tsp ground cinnamon

1 tsp ground ginger

½ tsp salt

2 cups sugar

2 large eggs

1 tsp vanilla extract

⅓ cup butter, melted and cooled

3-4 pears, peeled and diced, about 4 cups

*My grandma used to make a great fruit crisp, using pears or apples and a thin layer of topping that was just enough to cover the fruit with a sweet and crunchy contrast to the fruit below. This isn't quite like her recipe, but it definitely makes me think of her desserts. The cake is made with lots of pears and is barely held together with lightly spiced cake batter. There is quite a bit of sugar in this cake and, during baking, it forms a slight crust on top of the cake that really reminds me of grandma's fruit crisps.*

● ● ●

Preheat oven to 350F. Lightly grease a 9-inch square pan.

In a large bowl, sift together flour, baking powder, cinnamon, ginger, salt and sugar.

In a medium bowl whisk together eggs, vanilla and melted butter. Pour into dry ingredients and stir just until no streaks of flour remain. Stir in diced pears and pour into prepared baking pan.

Bake for 35-40 minutes until toothpick inserted into the center comes out clean and pears are tender.

Serve slightly warm, or at room temperature

*Serves 12*

# Pumpkin Spice Loaf

½ cup sugar

¾ cup brown sugar

1 large egg

¼ cup vegetable oil

¾ cup pumpkin puree

⅔ cup plain yogurt

1 tsp vanilla extract

1½ tsp ground cinnamon

1 tsp ground ginger

½ tsp ground cloves

¼ tsp ground allspice

¼ tsp freshly ground nutmeg

1½ cups all purpose flour

½ tsp baking soda

¼ tsp salt

*Although pumpkin paired with lots of rich spices is the perfect treat on a cool fall evening or cold winter morning, I don't think there is any reason to save this loaf for a particular time of year. A good cup of coffee is all you really need to accessorize this loaf. The pumpkin bread is spicy and sweet, with a great moist, dense texture that is reminiscent of pound cake. It also comes together very quickly. I always mix it up in one bowl and never spend more than 5 minutes from measuring everything out to getting the batter in the pan. Be sure to preheat the oven a few minutes in advance so that the loaf can go in as soon as it is ready.*

● ● ●

Preheat oven to 350F. Grease and flour a 9x5-inch loaf pan.

In a large bowl, whisk together sugars, egg, vegetable oil, pumpkin puree, yogurt, vanilla extract and all spices. Whisk until very smooth and all ingredients are well-incorporated.

Add in flour, baking soda and salt and whisk again until no streaks of dry ingredients remain and batter is fairly smooth.

Pour into prepared pan.

Bake for 55-60 minutes, or until a toothpick inserted into the center comes out clean.

Cool in pan for 10 minutes, then turn out onto a wire rack to cool completely.

*Makes 1 loaf*

# Vanilla Yogurt Coffee Cake

## Crumb Topping

⅔ cup all-purpose flour

⅓ cup sugar

⅓ cup chopped toasted pecans

⅛ tsp salt

¼ cup butter, melted and cooled

½ tsp vanilla extract


## Cake

1 cup sugar

½ cup butter, room temperature

1 tbsp vanilla extract

2 large eggs

2 cups all purpose flour

1 tsp baking powder

½ tsp baking soda

¼ tsp salt

1 cup plain Greek-style yogurt, low fat or full

*This is a great basic coffee cake, with a very moist vanilla-flavored cake made with yogurt in the batter. Plain, Greek-style yogurt is the best choice for this coffee cake. Greek yogurt is thicker and more like sour cream than other yogurts, with a nice, subtle tang to it. The topping is a simple one, without much spice to it. It has a subtle flavor of vanilla and has lots of pecans mixed in. The pecans toast up in the oven and take on a rich, nutty flavor as the cake bakes.*

● ● ●

Preheat oven to 350F. Grease a 9-in square pan.

**Make the Topping:** In a medium bowl, stir together flour, sugar, pecans and salt. Add in butter and vanilla and stir with a fork until wet crumbs are formed. Set aside.

**Make the Cake:** In a large bowl, cream together sugar and butter until light and fluffy. Beat in vanilla extract, then blend in the eggs one at a time.

In a medium bowl, whisk together flour, baking powder, baking soda and salt. Add to sugar mixture, alternating with sour cream in two or three additions, ending with an addition of the dry ingredients. Mix until batter is thick and no streaks of dry ingredients are visible. Pour into prepared pan and spread into an even layer. Top with streusel mixture, crumbling into an even layer with your fingertips.

Bake for 35-45 minutes or until toothpick inserted into the center comes out clean.

Cool on a wire rack for at least 30 minutes before slicing.

*Serves 12*

# Cinnamon Streusel Banana Cake

## Cake

1 ½ cups white whole wheat flour

½ cup sugar

½ cup brown sugar

1 tsp ground cinnamon

1 ½ tsp baking powder

¼ tsp salt

1 cup mashed banana
(2-3 medium bananas)

¼ cup vegetable oil

2 large eggs

1 tsp vanilla extract

½ cup chopped walnuts

## Streusel

½ cup sugar

¼ cup all purpose flour

1 tsp ground cinnamon

⅛ tsp salt

4 tbsp unsalted butter, melted

½ cup chopped walnuts

*I like the combination of whole wheat flour and bananas, since bananas seem to pick up on the nuttiness of the flour well. You might think that a cake with both of these elements would be dense, but this one is very light, moist and tender. The cake is actually great on its own, but to turn it into a coffee cake, a cinnamon crumb topping is added on. You can use whole wheat flour for the topping to remain consistent with the rest of the cake, but all purpose flour actually gives it a better flavor, since it is more neutral and lets the walnuts, butter and cinnamon stand out more.*

● ● ●

**Make the Cake:** Preheat oven to 350F and lightly grease a 9-inch round spingform pan.

In a large bowl, whisk together flour, sugars, cinnamon, baking powder and salt.

In a medium bowl, whisk together mashed banana, vegetable oil, eggs and vanilla until combined and smooth.

Pour into dry ingredients and stir until just combined and no streaks of flour remain. Stir in walnuts. Pour into prepared pan.

**Make the Topping:** In a small bowl, using an electric mixer on low speed, whisk together all topping ingredients until mixture is crumbly. Spread evenly over cake batter

Bake for 35-40 minutes, until a toothpick inserted into the center of the cake comes out clean.

Cool cake on a wire rack before slicing.

*Serves 12*

# Dark Chocolate Flecked Coffee Cake

## Streusel

²/₃ cup all-purpose flour

¹/₃ cup sugar

1-oz dark chocolate, shaved/finely chopped

¹/₈ tsp salt

¹/₄ cup butter, melted and cooled

¹/₂ tsp vanilla extract

## Cake

1 cup sugar

¹/₂ cup butter, room temperature

1 tbsp vanilla extract

2 large eggs

2 cups all purpose flour

1 tsp baking powder

¹/₂ tsp baking soda

¹/₄ tsp salt

1 cup sour cream

2-oz dark chocolate, shaved/finely chopped

*Adding chocolate to a coffee cake is an easy way to make chocolate an acceptable addition to any breakfast or brunch menu. This cake is actually a riff on my Vanilla Sour Cream Coffee Cake. It tones down the vanilla and adds chocolate shavings to both the cake and the streusel topping. I like chocolate shavings for a few reasons. First, they look very attractive in the cake itself. Second, you don't have to worry about them clumping together or sinking to the bottom of the cake, as chocolate chips tend to do. You end up with just a touch of chocolate in every bite. I use dark chocolate for this cake, but milk chocolate or semisweet chocolate will work well, too. Chocolate can be shaved off of a big block with a sharp knife or potato peeler, but you can get a similar effect by finely chopping up a bar of chocolate or by pulsing chocolate chips in a food processor.*

● ● ●

Preheat oven to 350F. Grease a 9-in square pan.

**Make the Topping:** In a medium bowl, stir together flour, sugar, chocolate shavings and salt. Add in butter and vanilla and stir with a fork until wet crumbs are formed. Set aside.

**Make the Cake:** In a large bowl, cream together sugar and butter until light and fluffy. Beat in vanilla extract, then blend in the eggs one at a time.

In a medium bowl, whisk together flour, baking powder, baking soda and salt. Add to sugar mixture, alternating with sour cream in two or three additions, ending with an addition of the dry ingredients. Mix until batter is thick and no streaks of dry ingredients are visible. Fold in chocolate shavings.

**Tip:** To shave chocolate, start with a block of chocolate and use a sharp knife to finely chop it. The chocolate will crack and turn into fine shards as you move the knife against one edge. You can also use a potato peeler to shave off pieces of chocolate into fine slivers, which is a great way to shave chocolate if you're worried about the knife slipping as you cut.

Pour into prepared pan and spread into an even layer. Top with streusel mixture, crumbling into an even layer with your fingertips.

Bake for 35-45 minutes or until toothpick inserted into the center comes out clean.

Cool on a wire rack for at least 30 minutes before slicing.

*Serves 12*

Muffins
& Scones

# Jelly Donut Muffins

1½ cups all purpose flour

2 tsp baking powder

¼ tsp salt

¼ tsp freshly ground nutmeg

¾ cup sugar

1 large egg

¼ cup vegetable oil

¾ cup buttermilk

1 tsp vanilla extract

¼ cup strawberry or raspberry jam

2 tbsp butter

½ cup sugar, for topping

*These muffins taste remarkably like donuts - without being fried. The donut effect comes from the fact that the muffins are rolled in sugar after baking, while the muffins are still hot. Brush a little melted butter on top of the muffins as soon as they come out of the oven, then roll the whole thing in the sugar. The muffin batter uses oil, not butter, and this makes the muffins soft and moist, so that the sugar adheres well to the sides and base without adding even more butter. There is also buttermilk, nutmeg and vanilla in the muffin batter, three flavors which evoke the taste of a classic cake donut. You can use any flavor of jam that you like to fill these muffins. My two favorites are raspberry and strawberry jam.*

• • •

Preheat oven to 350F. Lightly grease a 12-cup muffin tin (do not use paper liners for these muffins) with vegetable oil.

In a medium bowl, whisk together flour, baking powder, salt and nutmeg.

In a large bowl, whisk together sugar and egg until mixture is light in color. Stir in flour mixture, along with vegetable oil, milk and vanilla extract.

Drop a spoonful of batter into each muffin cup. Top with about a teaspoon of jam, then top with another spoonful of batter to cover the jam. Each should be ⅔ full.

Bake for 14-16 minutes, until a toothpick inserted into the center comes out clean.

While the muffins are baking, melt butter into a small bowl and pour remaining ½ cup sugar into a medium-sized bowl.

Remove the muffins from the pan one at a time. Dip the top of each muffin into the butter, then roll completely in sugar. Set on a wire rack to cool.

Serve warm or at room temperature.

*Makes 12*

**103**

# Blackberry Sour Cream Scones

2 cups all purpose flour

1 tsp baking powder

½ tsp baking soda

½ tsp salt

¼ cup sugar

6 tbsp butter, cold

¾ cup sour cream

1 cup blackberries, fresh or frozen

*These scones are moist and tender, a far cry from the hockey puck-like biscuits you'll find in some coffee shops, and a great favorite with skeptics who think that scones are generally too dry. The sour cream is the not-so-secret ingredient that keeps them soft and fresh tasting. Blackberries are great in these, not just because they taste good, but also because they add a beautiful purple-pink color scones. For variety you could try strawberries, raspberries and blueberries in these, too. I try to use fresh berries for these scones, but frozen work well, too.*

● ● ●

Preheat oven to 400F. Line a baking sheet with parchment paper.

Combine flour, baking powder, baking soda, salt and sugar in a large bowl. Cut butter into 4 or 5 chunks and add to flour mixture. Rub in butter with your fingertips until mixture resembles very coarse sand, with pieces of butter about the size of peas throughout. This step can also be done in a food processor.

Add in sour cream and mix until dough just starts to come together into a dry ball. Add in berries and knead dough gently with your hands until a moist dough forms. Try not to crush the berries too much.

Press ball of dough into a disc about 1-inch thick on a lightly floured surface. Use a sharp knife to divide dough into 8 wedges. Transfer to prepared baking sheet, leaving room for scones to spread slightly.

Bake for 18-20 minutes, until scones are lightly browned. Let the scones cool on the sheet for 5-10 minutes before serving.

*Makes 8*

# Buttermilk Scones

2 cup all purpose flour

1½ tsp baking powder

½ tsp baking soda

¼ tsp salt

¼ cup sugar

6 tbsp butter, cold and cut into small pieces

⅔ cup buttermilk

1 tsp vanilla

1 tbsp buttermilk, for topping
coarse sugar, for topping

*Buttermilk scones are plain, classic scones that are always a good choice. They're buttery, tender and go well with a whole variety of toppings, from jam to cream cheese to butter. To give them a finished look, brush them with a little bit of extra buttermilk and sprinkle them with coarse sugar before baking. This makes the tops of the scones slightly shiny, as well as adding a little sweet crunch to them.*

● ● ●

Preheat oven to 400F. Line a baking sheet with parchment paper.

In a large bowl, combine flour, baking powder, baking soda, salt and sugar and whisk to combine. Rub butter into the flour mixture with your fingers or a pastry cutter until the mixture resembles very coarse meal.

Stir in buttermilk and vanilla, adding the dried cherries as the dough starts to come together. The dough should be slightly sticky but not wet.

Divide dough in half and shape each into a disk that is about 1 inch thick. Place on prepared baking sheet and use a sharp knife to cut each disk into 5 wedges. Separate wedges slightly on baking sheet.

Using a pastry brush, brush tops with remaining 1 tbsp buttermilk and sprinkle liberally with coarse sugar.

Bake at 400F for 15-18 minutes, until lightly browned.

Transfer to a wire rack to cool. Scones can be served warm or at room temperature.

*Makes 10*

# Big Blueberry Lemon Muffins

3 cups all purpose flour

1 tbsp baking powder

½ tsp baking soda

½ tsp salt

⅓ cup butter, room temperature

¼ cup vegetable oil

1 cup sugar

2 large eggs

1 tsp vanilla extract

1 tbsp fresh lemon zest

1½ cups buttermilk

2 cups blueberries, fresh or frozen

*The trick to getting muffin tops that rise high above the rim of the pan is to use a thick batter and overfill the muffin cups. These muffins bake up to be tall, with beautifully domed tops. Fortunately, they're also moist and flavorful, too. A little bit of lemon really brightens up the blueberries in these muffins. Lemon extract is probably the easiest way to introduce a little bit of lemon, but you'll get the best flavor by using fresh lemon zest.*

● ● ●

Preheat oven to 375F. Line 16 muffin tin cups (might need two tins) with paper liners.

In a medium bowl, whisk flour, baking powder, baking soda and salt.

In a large bowl, cream together butter and sugar until light. Beat in the eggs one at a time, followed by the vegetable oil and the vanilla extract. Alternate buttermilk and flour into butter mixture, ending with an addition of flour and working in 2 or three additions. Stir in blueberries.

Divide batter evenly among muffin cups.

Bake for 18-22 minutes, until tops are lightly browned and a toothpick inserted into the center comes out clean.

Cool on a wire rack.

*Makes 16*

# Peach Bran Muffins

1 cup all purpose flour

½ cup oat bran

½ cup oat flour (oatmeal, finely ground)

¾ cup brown sugar

½ tsp baking powder

1 tsp baking soda

¼ tsp salt

½ tsp ground cinnamon

½ tsp ground cardamom

¼ tsp ground allspice

3 tbsp vegetable oil

⅔ cup unsweetened applesauce

1 large egg

¾ cup buttermilk

1½ cups diced peaches (2 medium)

*Dry, gritty and bland bran muffins are sadly prevalent, and they all serve to give bran muffins a bad reputation. Just like any other muffin, a bran muffin should be moist, tender and satisfying - and these are. They're even more moist than your average muffin and are fairly low in fat to boot. They're packed with oat bran, oat flour, applesauce and peaches. They're great with butter if you're going to eat them while lingering over coffee, but filling enough to make a good on-the-go breakfast. Oat flour is sold in natural food stores, but can be made at home by whizzing rolled oats in the food processor until finely ground.*

● ● ●

Preheat oven to 350F. Line a 12-cup muffin tin with paper liners.

In a large bowl, whisk together flour, oat bran, oat flour, baking powder, baking soda, salt and spices.

In a small bowl, whisk together vegetable oil, applesauce, egg and buttermilk. Pour into dry ingredients and stir until mixture is just combined and no streaks of flour remain. Stir in diced peaches.

Divide batter evenly into prepared muffin tin. Each cup should be filled just about to the top.

Bake for 15-17 minutes, until a toothpick inserted into the center comes out clean.

Cool on a wire rack before serving.

*Makes 12*

# Orange Chocolate Chip Scones

2 cups all purpose flour

1 tsp baking powder

¼ tsp baking soda

½ tsp salt

⅓ cup sugar

½ cup butter, chilled and

cut into 10-12 small pieces

8-10 tbsp fresh orange juice

2 tsp orange zest

¾ cup dark chocolate chips, divided

*Unlike many scone recipes, these don't need the addition of an extra butter or jam during serving to make them taste good. They are already bursting with flavor from a chocolate orange combination. The orange-flavored scones have both fresh orange zest and orange juice in them. Sweet orange juice is a good match for a slightly bitter dark chocolate, which is what I use in these scones. Chocolate chips alone are a good addition, but chocolate lovers might want to add even more chocolate by finishing these off with a drizzle of dark chocolate in addition to the chips.*

● ● ●

Preheat oven to 425F. Line a baking sheet with parchment paper.

In a medium bowl, whisk together flour, baking powder, baking soda, salt and sugar. Add butter and toss to coat. Using your finger tips, rub the butter into the flour mixture until it resembles very coarse sand, with no pieces large than a pea.

Add 5-6 tablespoons of orange juice and zest and stir dough with a fork. Add remaining juice until dough comes together into a not-too-moist ball. Stir in ½ cup chocolate chips.

Divide dough in to two balls, then divide each ball into four even pieces. Place each onto prepared baking sheet and press lightly until balls are about ¾-inch thick.

Bake for about 15 minutes, until scones are golden brown on top. Cool on a wire rack.

When scones are cooled, melt remaining ¼ cup chocolate in a small bowl in the microwave. Drizzle over cooled scones and let set before serving.

*Makes 8*

# Whole Wheat Banana Walnut Scones

## Scones

2¼ cups white whole wheat flour

⅓ cup brown sugar

2 tsp baking powder

½ tsp salt

½ tsp ground cinnamon

¼ tsp ground cloves

6 tbsp butter, chilled and cut into 6 pieces

½ cup banana, mashed

4-6 tbsp milk

½ cup chopped walnuts

## Cinnamon Glaze

1 cup confectioners' sugar

½ tsp ground cinnamon

½ tsp vanilla extract

2 tbsp milk

*Good scones are tender, not dense, an effect that can be difficult to achieve if you want to work some whole wheat flour into them. White whole wheat flour is a great ingredient in just this situation, since it produces a lighter scone than regular whole wheat, but still adds whole grains to the recipe. Mashed banana and chopped walnuts give these a banana bread-like flavor, and a cinnamon glaze adds some sweetness to the scones. If you can't get white whole wheat flour, a mixture of regular whole wheat and all purpose can be substituted.*

• • •

**Make the Scones:** Preheat oven to 400F. Line a baking sheet with parchment paper.

In a large bowl, whisk together flour, brown sugar, baking powder, salt and spices. Rub butter into flour mixture with your fingertips (or pulse in a food processor), mixing it in until no pieces larger than a pea remain. Stir in mashed banana, 4 tbsp milk and walnuts, adding additional milk as needed until dough comes together into a slightly sticky ball.

Divide dough in half and press each piece into a large disc about ¾-inch thick. Cut each disc into 5 equal pieces, making 10 total scones. Separate scones slightly on baking sheet.

Bake for 15-17 minutes, until edges are lightly browned.

Cool for at least 20 minutes, or to room temperature, on a wire rack before glazing.

**Make the glaze:** In a small bowl, whisk together confectioners' sugar, cinnamon, vanilla and milk. Drizzle over cooled scones before serving.

*Makes 10*

**115**

# Hazelnut Muffins

1 cup all purpose flour

1 cup white whole wheat flour

2 tsp baking powder

¼ tsp salt

½ cup hazelnut meal

½ cup sugar

½ cup brown sugar

2 large eggs

⅓ cup butter, melted and cooled

2 tsp vanilla extract

¾ cup milk

½ cup chopped hazelnuts

*These muffins are great for nut lovers. Hazelnut meal, which you can make by grinding hazelnuts in a food processor, adds a lovely dense, tender crumb to the muffin itself. Chopped hazelnuts make a great topping, as they toast up in the oven and add both flavor and a crunchy texture to the muffin. Since whole wheat flour has a bit of nuttiness to it, it works well in these muffins. White whole wheat flour keeps the batter lighter than regular whole wheat flour would, but both all purpose and regular whole wheat could be substituted.*

• • •

Preheat oven to 375F. Line 16 muffin cups with paper liners

In a medium bowl, whisk together flours, baking powder and salt.

In a large bowl, whisk together hazelnut meal, sugars, eggs, melted butter and vanilla extract. Add half of the flour mixture to the hazelnut mixture, followed by the milk. Stir in the remaining flour mixture, mixing only until no streaks of dry ingredients remain.

Divide batter evenly into 16 muffin cups, filling each about ¾ full. It is fine if the muffins need to be baked in two batches due to lack of oven space; the batter sitting out for a few extra minutes will still bake up well.

Top each muffin with about ½ tbsp chopped hazelnuts.

Bake for 15-17 minutes, until a toothpick inserted into the center comes out clean.

Cool muffins on a wire rack.

*Makes 16*

# Citrus Sour Cream Muffins

## Muffin

2 ¼ cups all purpose flour

2 tsp baking powder

½ tsp salt

6 tbsp butter, room temperature

¾ cup sugar

1 large egg

1 tbsp orange zest

1 tbsp lemon zest

¼ cup lemon juice

¼ cup orange juice

¾ cup sour cream

## Topping

⅓ cup coarse sugar

1 tbsp lemon juice

1 tbsp orange juice

When it comes to citrus flavors, you can't have too much of a good thing. These muffins have both lemon and orange juices in them, as well as lemon and orange zests. On top of that, literally, is a glaze made with the same pair of juices and some sugar. The glaze is a little unusual in that it uses coarse sugar, instead of confectioners' sugar. It leaves a little bit of a crunch of sugar on top of each muffin and the juice is absorbed right into the muffin itself, adding some extra moisture and flavor. Tangy sour cream also helps keep the muffins moist, and complements the acidity of the citrus.

● ● ●

**Make the muffins:** Preheat the oven to 400F. Line a 12-cup muffin tin with paper liners.

In a medium bowl, whisk together flour, baking powder and salt.

In a large bowl, cream together butter and sugar until fluffy. Beat in egg and orange and lemon zests.

Stir in about ⅓ of the flour mixture to the butter mixture, followed by the lemon and orange juices. Stir in additional ⅓ of the flour mixture, followed by the sour cream. Mix in remaining flour and stir just until no streaks of dry ingredients remain. Batter will be thick.

Divide batter evenly into prepared muffin cups; the cups may be slightly overfilled.

Bake for 15-17 minutes, until a toothpick inserted into the center comes out clean. Turn out onto a wire rack to glaze and cool

**Make the glaze:** While muffins are baking, whisk together all topping ingredients in a small bowl.

Drizzle a teaspoonful over each muffin as soon as it comes out of the oven, while the muffins are still hot.

*Makes 12*

Index